THE SEARCH FOR MEANING

Ecclesiastes

by Tim McMahon

MATTHIAS MEDIA

The Search for Meaning
© Tim McMahon, 2001

Matthias Media

THE GOOD BOOK COMPANY
Elm House, 37 Elm Road
New Malden, Surrey KT3 3HB
Tel: 020-8942-0880
Fax: 020-8942-0990
e-mail: admin@thegoodbook.co.uk
Website: www.thegoodbook.co.uk

Unless otherwise indicated, Scripture taken from the HOLY BIBLE, NEW INTERNATIONAL VERSION. Copyright © 1973, 1978, 1984 International Bible Society. Used by permission of Zondervan Bible Publishers.

ISBN 1 876326 32 8
All rights reserved. Except as may be permitted by the Copyright Act, no part of this publication may be reproduced in any form or by any means without prior permission from the publisher.

Cover illustration by Kirsty McAllister

Contents

How to make the most of these studies 4

1 First impressions (Eccles 12:8-14) 7

2 When wisdom fails (Eccles 1) 15

3 What to conclude when you can't reach a conclusion (Eccles 2) 21

4 How to cope when life doesn't make sense (Eccles 3) 27

5 The sacrifice of fools (Eccles 4:1-5:7) 33

6 The root of all meaninglessness (Eccles 5:8-6:12; 8:1-17) 39

7 Why we can't find the meaning of life (Eccles 7) 47

8 Why we should live life to the full (Eccles 9:1-11:6) 57

9 The end of the matter (Eccles 11:7-12:14) 65

How to make the most of these studies

1. What is an Interactive Bible Study?

These 'interactive' Bible studies are a bit like a guided tour of a famous city. The studies will take you through Ecclesiastes, pointing out things along the way, filling in background details, and suggesting avenues for further exploration. But there is also time for you to do some sight-seeing of your own–to wander off, have a good look for yourself, and form your own conclusions.

In other words, we have designed these studies to fall half-way between a sermon and a set of unadorned Bible study questions. We want to provide stimulation and input and point you in the right direction, while leaving you to do a lot of the exploration and discovery yourself.

We hope that these studies will stimulate lots of 'interaction'– interaction with the Bible, with the things we've written, with your own current thoughts and attitudes, with other people as you discuss them, and with God as you talk to him about it all.

2. The format

Each study contains sections of text to introduce, summarize, suggest and provoke. We've left plenty of room in the margins for you to jot comments and questions as you read. Interspersed throughout the text are three types of 'interaction', each with their own symbol:

For starters

Questions to break the ice and get you thinking.

Investigate

Questions to help you investigate key parts of the Bible.

Think it Through

Questions to help you think through the implications of your discoveries and write down your own thoughts and reactions.

When you come to one of these symbols, you'll know that it's time to do some work of your own. Each study also concludes with some suggestions for prayer.

3. Suggestions for Individual Study

- Before you begin, pray that God would open your eyes to what he is saying in Ecclesiastes and give you the spiritual strength to do something about it. You may be spurred to pray again at the end of the study.
- Work through the study, following the directions as you go. Write in the spaces provided.
- Resist the temptation to skip over the *Think it through* sections. It is important to think about the sections of text (rather than just accepting them as true) and to ponder the implications for your life. Writing these things down is a very valuable way to get your thoughts working.
- Take what opportunities you can to talk to others about what you've learnt.

4. Suggestions for Group Study

- Much of the above applies to group study as well. The studies are suitable for structured Bible study or cell groups, as well as for more informal pairs and threesomes. Get together with a friend/s and work through them at your own pace; use them as the basis for regular Bible study with your spouse. You don't need the formal structure of a 'group' to gain maximum benefit.
- It is *vital* that group members work through the study themselves *before* the group meets. The group discussion can take place comfortably in an hour (depending on how sidetracked you get!), but only if all the members have done the work and are familiar with the material.
- Spend most of the group time discussing the 'interactive' sections—*Investigate* and *Think it through*. Reading all the text together will take too long and should be unnecessary if the group members have done their preparation. You may wish to underline and read aloud particular paragraphs or sections of text that you think are important.
- The role of the group leader is to direct the course of the discussion and to try to draw the threads together at the end. This will mean a little extra preparation—underlining important sections of text to emphasize, working out which questions are worth concentrating on, and being sure of the main thrust of the study. Leaders will also probably want to work out approximately how long they'd like to spend on each part.
- We haven't included an 'answer guide' to the questions in the studies. This is a deliberate move. We want to give you a guided tour of Ecclesiastes, not a lecture. There is more than enough in the text we have written and the questions we have asked to point you in what we think is the right direction. The rest is up to you.

1
First impressions

"Meaningless! Meaningless!" says the Teacher. "Utterly meaningless! Everything is meaningless."

So begins and ends the book of Ecclesiastes. And on twenty-eight occasions in between, the author exclaims that particular things are meaningless; things which are greatly valued by most people—like work, education, relationships, even life itself. How can such a bleak view of life be reconciled with genuine faith in God? Is there truth in the charge that Ecclesiastes is actually atheistic in outlook? If so, what is the book doing in the Bible?

A cursory study of Ecclesiastes lays to rest the suspicion that it might be atheistic in outlook. For a start, there are more than 30 references to God in the book, and they are not negative references. The author clearly believes in God, and urges his readers to fear God (e.g. 5:7; 7:18; 12:13). To be sure, he comes to unsettling conclusions as he struggles with the contradictions and absurdities that life throws at us, but he comes to these conclusions as a believer. Here is the first clue as to why the book is in the Bible: to help believers reconcile their belief in God with the confounding experiences of life.

For Starters

1. How much thought have you given to questions like: "Why have faith in God when so much in life seems pointless or even unjust?" What conclusions have you come to?

2. Apart from the personal benefit that might come from gaining a deeper understanding of God and the world in which we live, how might grappling with this issue help us engage with others?

Great ones have addressed this issue at length, and possibly none greater than Solomon–the wisest, wealthiest, grandest king in Israel's history. Solomon has traditionally been taken as the author of Ecclesiastes, and we find no good reason to depart from this view. Even if we find his conclusions shocking, we should be very wary of dismissing them, because he is uniquely qualified to pronounce on the matter. We will investigate two reasons why his conclusions should carry great weight.

Investigate

1. The author points out twice in the opening chapter that he is the king of Jerusalem, sitting on David's throne (1:1,12). Look up the following passages and note the promise God makes to Solomon, the first son of David to succeed his father. To what extent was the promise fulfilled?

   1 Kings 3:7-14

   1 Kings 4:29-34

2. Note the response of people to Solomon in 1 Kings 4:34. What should be our attitude to the writings of such a king? Should we expect such writings to support an atheistic worldview?

3. What else resulted from Solomon's wisdom (1 Kings 10:23-25)? How would this affect his ability to conduct a major research project?

The great wealth and wisdom of Solomon qualifies him above all others to undertake the research project which is the book's chief subject. If Solomon cannot find answers, no-one can. The magnitude of his project is as breath-taking as the magnitude of his wealth and wisdom. He sets out to discover the meaning of life.

His findings are of interest to the whole world—1 Kings 10 records the Queen of Sheba travelling from Africa to hear

Solomon's wisdom. The name traditionally ascribed to the book, 'Ecclesiastes', derives from the Greek word meaning 'assembly' or 'meeting'. It reflects the apparent purpose of the book: to present to a great assembly the findings of the most important research project in the world—the quest for the meaning of life. The title the author of Ecclesiastes uses of himself also conveys this 'public speaking' function—it is variously translated in English versions of the Bible as 'the Teacher', 'the Preacher', 'the Philosopher'. If he were presenting his findings at a major convention today, he might be billed as 'the Keynote Speaker'. For the purposes of this study, we will follow the NIV translation of "Teacher".

At first glance, his great research project seems to be a failure. The recurring verdict is that everything is "meaningless" (as the NIV puts it). This is quite a good translation of the Hebrew word *hebel* that keeps popping up throughout Ecclesiastes. But it could also be misleading if by it we think the Teacher is concluding that there is no meaning to anything at all. As we shall see, his conclusion is not that there is no meaning, but that ultimate meaning is impossible for even the richest and wisest researcher to discover. His quest has been futile. Other English translations of the Bible use words like 'vanity' or 'futility' to reflect this nuance.

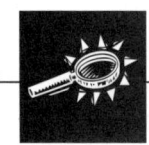

Investigate

1. We can begin to get a feel for the message of Ecclesiastes and form some first impressions by reading the whole book through in one sitting. The three questions below will help you keep focussed while you read.

If you are doing these studies in a group, you might like to divide into pairs or threesomes. Each of these sub-groups can take a different section of the book, read through it, discuss the questions, and then report back to the main group.
   ★ Ecclesiastes 1:1-2:26
   ★ Ecclesiastes 3:1-5:7
   ★ Ecclesiastes 5:8-8:17
   ★ Ecclesiastes 9:1-12:14

a. In what areas of life does the Teacher conclude there is no hope of finding meaning? Who or what is responsible for this?

b. What responses to life does the Teacher describe?

c. Where does God fit into the Teacher's conclusions?

Now look more closely at the Teacher's conclusion in Ecclesiastes 12:9-14.

2. Given the Teacher's wider literary reputation described in 12:9-10, what should we expect about the orderliness of argument and the ease of comprehension of this book? Is your first impression of the book consistent with such an expectation? Be honest!

3. If the form of the book in some way reflects the subject it **examines**, what would you conclude about our ability to come to a deep **understanding** of that subject?

At first reading, the Teacher's conclusion seems bleak indeed: our search for meaning is futile, and our efforts to find it will all be in vain. We cannot make sense of "life under the sun"; we cannot see into its meaning. It is opaque to us.

But it is not a completely negative conclusion. It does leave open the possibility that we might be able to discover the ultimate meaning of life if the impediments to our gaining of knowledge are dealt with–though the Teacher does not give us any reason to expect them to be lifted. But at least he has pointed out the problems that must be dealt with if meaning is ever to become accessible to human beings. Before we can benefit from this knowledge, we must first be willing to accept the Teacher's negative conclusions. We need to think through why we might be reluctant to do this.

Think it through

1. Thinking about your life in general, to what extent would you say it has been:
   - satisfying and fulfilling?
   - frustrating?
   - incomprehensible?
   - boring?
   - possessing a sense of purpose and direction?

   Why?

2. Our predisposition to be optimistic or pessimistic will affect the response we make to the message of Ecclesiastes. At one end of the spectrum are 'happy optimists'–people for whom life is something to be upbeat about, who view problems as being put to right, and who tend to ignore or downplay even obvious evil. At the other end are 'miserable pessimists' who cannot escape the disturbing

> realities of evil and injustice, who do not see matters improving, and who find the world a predominantly unhappy and disordered place. Where would you put yourself on this spectrum? Where would you put the message of Ecclesiastes?
>
> Happy Optimist   Miserable Pessimist
>
> _____
>
> 3. How willing are you to be told that you cannot find the meaning of life; that you are incapable of searching out an answer? What makes this proposition such a bitter pill for us to swallow, regardless of our predisposition to optimism or pessimism?

If we are to benefit from the book of Ecclesiastes, we must not move too quickly to New Testament passages which seem to offer answers to the problems the Teacher raises. We must first let the truth of what the Teacher is saying really penetrate our minds. Until we confront the unvarnished truth of what life is like "under the sun", we cannot even begin to appreciate the solace held out in the rest of the gospel message. We need to learn that the only appropriate response to our condition is to fear God in the midst of it. We should be willing to humbly depend upon God and not demand that the world or our lives be comprehensible to us. Then we will have the right attitude to be able to accept whatever solace God may offer us in the New Testament. In short, the message of Ecclesiastes will help us 'live by faith'. This, of course, is the ultimate purpose of all Scripture.

Pray

1. Confess those areas of life in which you are sorely tempted to demand an explanation from God as to why he lets things happen the way they do.

2. Pray that you will increasingly develop an attitude of humble dependence on God through these studies.

2

Ecclesiastes 1
When wisdom fails

The book of Ecclesiastes is often grouped with the Old Testament books of Job, Proverbs and Song of Songs as 'wisdom literature', and for good reason. Ecclesiastes not only has the literary character of 'wisdom literature', but 'wisdom' itself is one of its major subjects. What does it mean to be wise? What is the difference between 'biblical wisdom' and 'worldly wisdom'? And what should we conclude when the very best of our wisdom is inadequate? Let's start by identifying what we mean when we say someone is 'wise'.

For starters

1. What does it mean to say that someone is 'street-wise'? In what sense can kids who have dropped out of school long before getting a 'proper' education be considered wise?

2. What would show that a stockbroker is wise? How important would academic qualifications be in your assessment?

3. Name some people you think are wise. What is it about them that makes you consider them to be wise?

Wise people are able to take into account the way things really are in the world, and order their lives around that reality. They tend to get ahead in life, to live successfully. Rather than being idealists who are unable to accommodate reality because they think 'things shouldn't be this way', wise people are realists who might not like the way the world is, but accept it and live accordingly. They are able to fit in, and make the most of the circumstances. To be wise is to live according to reality.

This is true of both worldly wisdom and biblical wisdom. The difference between them is their scope. To be wise in a biblical sense is to see reality painted on the broadest possible canvas: it is to acknowledge that God exists, is involved in the world, and that we live in relationship to him, to his creation and to each other. The truly wise person will take God into account when choosing how to live "life under the sun". So the catch-cry of the biblical wisdom literature is: "the fear of the Lord is the beginning of wisdom" (e.g. Prov 1:7).

Think it Through

1. Many would consider knowledge of God as unnecessary to be truly wise. Some would even see spiritual beliefs as a hindrance to being wise. Why might people think this way?

> 2. Can someone be an atheist and still be wise?

The book of Ecclesiastes brings all the resources of biblical wisdom to the task of trying to make sense of life. What is it all for? Why is one course in life better than another? Can we find a fundamental meaning or purpose that makes life intelligible and satisfying? To put the question in its simplest form: 'Why?'

This is a question that humanity has always asked. Young children have a particular tendency to ask it of the most impossible subjects. If a credible answer is to be proposed which will command universal respect, it will likely only arise after extensive research and careful reflection. It needs to be addressed by someone with great resources, both intellectual and experiential. But it is also a question that needs to be tackled in a down-to-earth, practical way. The findings should be widely distributed, not locked up in inaccessible tomes that only academics will read.

Ecclesiastes seeks to do all this. It reads like a great researcher presenting his findings to a public gallery after years of painstaking investigation. No budget was set for this research, no expense spared, no stone left unturned. The presentation of the results is not dry and indigestible, but reads like a good work of popular science journalism. The author clearly knows his subject, and yet is able to communicate to a mass audience. The writer of Ecclesiastes is a master of wit and pithy sayings; he takes us on a roller-coaster ride of emotions; he communicates with intriguing anecdotes, beautiful poetry and dogmatic conclusions; he compels us to unavoidable conclusions by rigorous argument. The book of Ecclesiastes is clearly no ordinary philosophical work. It is the God-inspired wisdom of history's pre-eminent sage on the grandest of subjects. We should expect to benefit immensely from serious study of it.

However, what if we were to find that, in the end, this pre-eminently wise researcher failed in his quest? What if the cleverest and most well-resourced wise-man in history found that his wisdom was not much use?

As chapter 1 lays out the basic shape of the Teacher's research program, this is the awful possibility that is raised.

Investigate

Read Ecclesiastes 1:2-18.

1. What is the Teacher's opening theory about life?

2. How does he explain and illustrate this theory (in vv. 3-11)?

3. The Teacher clearly has a perceptive understanding of the natural world (as vv. 4-7 show). But what impression does he give of humanity's ability to deeply penetrate the meaning of things?

4. What is the researcher's investigative method, and its scope (v.13)?

5. What is his initial conclusion (v. 14)? The word traditionally translated "vanity" in verses 2 and 14 (NIV "meaningless") basically means 'vapour' or 'breath'. Having looked over chapter 1, what do you think the Teacher means by saying that life under the sun is "meaningless"?

6. The Teacher considers that perhaps his method of study—wisdom—is the wrong way to go about this research. What is his conclusion about the effectiveness of the opposite approach—foolishness (vv. 16-17)?

7. What does the Teacher say is the appropriate response to this conclusion (v. 18)?

In an age when 'university tests prove...' and every problem is deemed solvable by just doing a bit more research or developing some new technology, the words of the Teacher are a slap in the face. They remind us proud moderns that for all our sophistication and cleverness, any human attempt to find 'the meaning of life' is futile; that the bitter reality of death mocks us all.

Sadly, many Christians today seek diversion from this truth, rather than learning from Scripture how to deal with it. Maybe the best illustration of this in recent times was the funeral of Diana, Princess of Wales, following her tragic death in August 1997. It was estimated that over a billion people worldwide watched the funeral service on television. All who saw the coffin bearing the 37-year-old princess were confronted with the futility of life in the face of death. The church leaders presiding at her funeral had the opportunity to help a sixth of the world's population face up to this harsh reality. All they had to do was read and explain a passage of Scripture which did this—like Jesus' words about the collapse of the Tower of Siloam in Luke 13:1-5, or almost any part of Ecclesiastes. Instead, the sentimental favourite 'Ode to Love' from 1 Corinthians 13 was read, with no explanation of its context. People were moved and became dewy-eyed, but no-one heard the word of God which so powerfully addressed the situation. An unparalleled opportunity went begging. Maybe the church leaders just lost their nerve; more troubling is the possibility that they did not know the word of God which addresses our human condition.

In later studies we will find out what further wisdom the Teacher can shed on the issue of the futility of life. But before we move on from chapter 1, let us join with him in feeling (rather than avoiding) the sorrow and grief associated with not being able to penetrate the meaning of "life under the sun".

Think it through

1. Looking at the world, and at the events of your own life, what would lead you to a similar conclusion to the Teacher (i.e. that life is pointless, meaningless, futile)?

2. How does it make you feel? How do you normally deal with (or shield yourself from) those feelings?

3. Look up Romans 8:18-25 and Matthew 5:4. When is it appropriate for believers to mourn and groan, and why? What will be the ultimate outcome, and when?

Pray

1. Pray that God will make you more willing to experience the godly grief that should accompany our inability to understand the meaning of life and the events of life.

2. Pray that your church and your group will develop a culture of realism about the profound sorrow people can experience in life, and provide proper support that does not deny the perplexity of life for people going through such grief.

3. Pray for particular people you know who may be experiencing such sorrow at this time.

3

Ecclesiastes 2

What to conclude when you can't reach a conclusion

In chapter 2 of Ecclesiastes, the Teacher takes his readers through a full phase of his investigation by wisdom of "life under the sun". He looks at pleasure and possessions, at wisdom and work. He leaves us with the valuable lesson: what to conclude when you can't reach a conclusion.

Investigate

1. Briefly summarise the aspects of "life under the sun" investigated by the Teacher.

   2:1-3

   2:4-6

   2:7-9

   2:10

2. What is his conclusion at the end of these extensive investigations (v. 11)?

3. As any good Teacher would do after drawing a blank from careful study, the author of Ecclesiastes evaluates his research method (wisdom), and the sufficiency of the effort he put into his research (v. 12). Why does he conclude that wisdom should not be abandoned?

4. What great event makes neither wisdom nor foolishness any better than the other in absolute terms for discovering the meaning of life (vv. 14-16)?

5. What are the Teacher's responses to this conclusion? How strong are the words used to describe these responses? Who is involved in each response?

    Negatively (vv. 17-23)

    Positively (vv. 24-26)

6. How are the Teacher's conclusions—both the positive and negative ones—consistent with reality? That is, how are they wise?

Despite the futility the Teacher feels after all his effort, he doesn't abandon God or spit in his face. Rather, he is content to enjoy whatever good he can find in his meaningless life. He wants us to follow his example, without swallowing the world's lie that such enjoyment is the purpose of life.

Like the Teacher, we should be willing to enter fully into the experience of profound sadness when it is thrust upon us by the events of life. We should not deny that things are genuinely bad. We should not demand that God explain the purpose of every instance of suffering we or others go through. We should not manufacture a falsely upbeat spirituality to dull the pain of not being able to penetrate the meaning of life. This understanding of the world—that there may be meaning to life, but God is denying us the ability to fathom it—provides the strength to live in a perplexing world.

Godly believers, far from being ones who live with an unrealistic worldview, should be the ones who blow the whistle on the spurious meanings of life that so many in our world cling to. The results of the Teacher's research can be used to challenge their purpose for living. Some may see the vaporous nature of their outlook on life, and be willing to give consideration to a more honest alternative.

Think it through

1. Many people today seek to find meaning in the kinds of ways Solomon did. Fill in the following table:

Attempts to find meaning	In what specific ways do people today try to find meaning in these pursuits?	How would you challenge them with the ultimate futility of doing so?
the pursuit of pleasure/fun		
using alcohol to make life enjoyable		
involvement in great projects, pursuing great achievements		
the gathering of possessions		
the constant quest for greater sexual fulfilment		
the pursuit of wisdom and intellectual endeavour		

2. Which of these pursuits are most appealing to you? Are there any matters here in which you need to change your attitude and/or behaviour?

3. Christians are often portrayed as wowsers or kill-joys, unable to enjoy life, and not wanting others to either. How does the message of Ecclesiastes 1-2 free Christians from a kill-joy approach to life? Yet how does it also give us reason to restrain from doing whatever we like in life? Which extreme do you think is the greater danger for Christians today?

Christians often jump to the apostle Paul to provide an antidote to the Teacher's pessimism about the futility of life in the face of death. But Paul seems to share the Teacher's verdict about life and death.

Read 1 Corinthians 15:12-19, 50-58.

4. How does Paul echo the same sentiments as the Teacher on the futility of life and even of Christian faith if death truly is the end?

5. How does the expectation of physical resurrection deal with the problem of death the Teacher so forcibly confronts us with throughout Ecclesiastes?

Pray

1. Pray that we will have the humility to accept the Teacher's conclusion about our inability to find the meaning of life.

2. Pray for yourself and your church that you will demonstrate the joy, the humility, and the realism of living according to Ecclesiastes' view of life.

3. Pray that you will not live as a libertine or a wowser.

4. Pray that you will have opportunities to challenge particular people you know who hold inadequate views of the purpose of life.

4

Ecclesiastes 3

How to cope when life doesn't make sense

If we are honest, everyone feels at times that life doesn't make sense. Christians are no exception. But Christians sometimes feel it would be wrong to suggest that life is incomprehensible, unjust or out of control. While everyone has to struggle to cope when life doesn't make sense, many Christians have the additional burden of trying to keep up the right face before other Christians. It can make life that much harder.

For starters

1. What situations in your life have left you asking "Why? What is the point of it? Why has God allowed this to happen?" Did you articulate these feelings to other Christians? Why or why not? If you did, how were they received?

2. How do you cope in such situations? What thoughts go through your mind? How do you reconcile them with your faith in God?

The middle chapters of Ecclesiastes contain some of the most beautiful and oft-quoted words in the book, and yet also some of the most despairing. In chapter 3 we plunge from the literary heights of an inspirational poem on time, to a clinical comparison of dead animals and human corpses. Despite the Teacher's ability to capture the ebb and flow of time in poetry, he laments our inability to fathom what happens after we die. The chapter concludes with an acknowledgement of the impenetrable wall to knowledge of the future posed by death. The message is ultimately quite despairing.

Yet ever since The Byrds made Ecclesiastes 3:1-8 famous in their song 'Turn! Turn! Turn!', it has been customary to see this passage as evoking a very positive view of life and the cosmos. This outlook is more in sympathy with the spirit of the 60s and its benign sense of oneness with the universe, than with the brutal honesty of the Teacher who sees God as set against us. Not that the Teacher's conclusions have all been negative thus far—he has found that wisdom is better than foolishness, and that God can give satisfaction in life through work. But he has also observed that both the wise and the foolish suffer the same ultimate fate—death—and that we have to leave the fruits of our labour to someone else, who may turn out to be a complete idiot. He is forced to the conclusion that, from our point of view, everything is meaningless. Not the sort of lyric that is likely to top the charts.

Investigate

Read Ecclesiastes 3:1-15.

1. The form of the poem about time—its rhythm and repetition, its ebb and flow—reflects its subject matter. There is a time for everything in the ebb and flow of life under the sun (vv.1-8). How does this observation fit into the Teacher's thought up to this point in the book?

2. What does the Teacher say we can, and cannot, work out in all our toiling at understanding (vv. 9-11)?

3. Who does he say is responsible for this situation?

4. If this is the way things are, what should be our attitude to the good times when they come our way (vv. 12-13)? How does this conclusion tie in with the conclusions of 2:24-26?

5. How does the truth about God asserted in v.14a contrast with the truth about ourselves repeated so many times in the book so far?

6. Why has God made things this way (v. 14)?

7. In verses 16-22, note down:

   - the two things the Teacher observes about the world

   - the two things the Teacher says about God

   - his conclusion

In chapter 3 the Teacher makes it clear that God has appointed a time for everything that happens, whether birth or death, keeping or finding, war or peace. Everything has its appropriate or right time in his scheme of things (v. 11). The problem is, we do not have access to his scheme of things.

This is the burden God has placed on us: we remember the past and think about the future, and so are acutely aware of the inconsistencies and injustices of life. This is most likely what the word 'eternity' means in v.11–God has set a notion of the whole span of time in our hearts–'the past, the present, and the future'. Even so, we cannot fathom the overall workings of God to make sense of it all. The most we can do is to enjoy the good times when they come, knowing they are from God at his appointed time. But this does not provide an overall rationale for the events of life, any more than do the bad times when they inexplicably come. God has made things this way for a very good reason: so that we will fear him. The NIV uses the slightly weaker English word "revere" in v. 14, but in the original it is the normal word for 'fear'. God's intention is to humble us by confounding us. And he is willing to let us go through profound personal suffering so that we will learn the lesson.

This teaching is so abhorrent to us that we want to deny it. We need to ponder our own expectations to understand why we find these lessons so hard to accept.

Think it through

1. When something good happens to you, what sort of conclusion do you usually come to?

- God is blessing me because I am one of his children.

- God is rewarding me for the good things I do.

- Aren't I worthy to have had this happen to me?

- Some other reaction:

2. What would be the reaction of the Teacher?

3. When something bad happens to you, what sort of conclusion do you usually come to?

   - God isn't really in control, or else he wouldn't let this happen.

   - God is punishing me for my sin.

   - What did I do to deserve this?

   - This is all my fault; I should have seen this coming and avoided it somehow.

   - Some other reaction:

4. What would be the reaction of the Teacher?

5. How might the Teacher's conclusions—which he comes to as a believer—call into question the commonly held view that Christians can discern God's will for their lives by reflecting upon and praying about the circumstances and events of life?

6. Contrary to popular belief, Jesus used parables to stop people from finding meaning, rather than to illumine people. Look up Matthew 13:10-16. Those who were willing to accept that they could not fathom spiritual truths themselves would pursue Jesus for revelation (v. 16). Those who were not willing to accept this would be confirmed in their unbelief.

Could we use the message of Ecclesiastes in our evangelism in a similar way that Jesus used parables to sift his hearers? Would it be right for us to do this?

7. How might the message of Ecclesiastes play a part in commending the Christian faith to someone who is genuinely searching for the meaning of life?

Pray

1. Pray that God will give you a deep conviction of his right to order all things in his world as he sees fit, and that he is under no obligation to reveal to you the reasons why incomprehensible and often incredibly painful events happen in your life.

2. Pray for anyone you know who is going through a particularly difficult time at present which may be causing them to demand answers from God. Pray that these times will lead them to a deeper acknowledgment of the rightness of humbly depending on God, even when life doesn't make sense.

3. Also pray that you will be able to rejoice with thanksgiving in those times which bring a sense of satisfaction and enjoyment in life. Give thanks with anyone in your group who has reason for such rejoicing at present.

5

Ecclesiastes 4:1-5:7

The sacrifice of fools

So far in Ecclesiastes, we have seen the Teacher investigating, researching and pondering the nature of life under the sun. He still has more work to do, but already he has begun to outline his view of the world and of God. As we saw in our last study, he does not question the sovereign rule of God, nor God's right to do as he sees fit in his world. However, he strongly asserts that we are not God. We do not understand what is going on. We cannot give a meaningful rationale for the past, and we don't know what is going to happen in the future. The wise person realises this and lives accordingly, enjoying what God gives, and fearing him. But not everyone is wise.

Investigate

Read Ecclesiastes 4:1-16.

1. What is the Teacher's reaction to the oppression he sees in the world?

2. How does this fit in with his views outlined in chapters 2 and 3?

3. In verses 4-8, he turns his attention to human work and labour. What four attitudes towards work does he describe?

•

•

•

•

4. Which of these attitudes does he commend? How does this fit in with his overall philosophy of life?

5. Why are two better than one (vv. 9-12)?

6. In verses 13-16, the obvious truth that wisdom is 'better' than foolishness is both reinforced and undercut. How? In the light of 1:12-14, what might the Teacher expect to become of his wisdom?

At first glance, this chapter seems to be a mishmash of different subjects, but one perspective lies behind them all. This perspective is the one that we have already met in chapters 1-3, namely that some things are better than others in life, and should be enjoyed, but that this still doesn't help us understand the meaninglessness of what happens. It is the message of chapter 3 verse 22:

So I saw that there is nothing better for a man than to enjoy his work, because that is his lot. For who can bring him to see what will happen after him?

The wise person therefore works in a way that allows him to enjoy his toil. He avoids the error of laziness, which leads to ruin (4:5), but he also sees the folly of over-work. Better to have a little less and enjoy it in tranquillity, than to be ruined by ambition, striving and envy. Here is a timely challenge for our ambitious, striving, workaholic society. Better, the Teacher might say, to drive your kids around in an old Ford than to drive to see them on custody visits in a current model BMW. Better a happy home on one income, than a stressed and chaotic one on two. Better a crowded, run-down cottage where there is love than a mansion where there is loneliness.

The Teacher here touches on one of those fundamentally good aspects of life in God's creation: relationships. If you want to enjoy the life God has allotted to you under the sun, then you will enjoy and profit more from it with someone else than on your own. Nor is he just talking about marriage—in fact, brothers, sons and friends are the relationships specifically mentioned in verses 8-10.

Think it through

1. Where do you see examples of the foolish attitudes to work and ambition described in Ecclesiastes 4:

- among people you know?

- in your own life?

So far, the Teacher has been saying that to respond appropriately to the way life is, there are two basic things to do:
   a. enjoy whatever you can, as the gift of God, and
   b. fear God

Having expanded a little on the enjoyment of God's gifts in chapter 4, he turns in the first part of chapter 5 to the fear of God.

Investigate

Read Ecclesiastes 5:1-7.

1. How would you summarize the attitude towards God in this passage?

2. How should this attitude affect:
   - our listening?

   - our speech?

Most of what is said in these verses focuses on words. The Teacher commends listening to God's words over doing sacrificial actions (5:1). He warns against not fulfilling our word when we promise to do something, because God sees all (5:4). He exhorts us twice to be few in words when we speak to God, but to listen much, because of the insignificance of our words compared to his (5:2,7). Standing in awe of God (again, the phrase is simply 'fear God' in 5:7) means being humble before him, being aware of the relative enormity of his importance, power and knowledge compared to ours. It means listening to his words and offering few of our own, especially when meeting with God's people in "the house of God".

Think it through

1. In many churches today, the activity of 'worship' is synonymous with times of singing and spontaneous prayer. The more heartfelt, and often the more extended these times of singing and prayer, the 'better' the worship is said to be. On the other hand, in some Christian mystical traditions, utter silence and personal meditation, ideally in a 'holy place', is considered to be the best way to worship God. Only then can deep communion with God be entered into. What would the Teacher say to each of these views?

2. How should Ecclesiastes 5:1-7 affect what we do in church today?

3. In Colossians 3:15-17, Paul addresses what Christians are to do when we meet together, and how the relationship with God so nurtured should affect all the other activities we do in life. How does the Teacher's message so far in Ecclesiastes shed light on these New Testament verses?

Pray

1. Pray that your understanding will grow of the enormity of God and the significance of his words compared to ours.

2. Pray that you will give more and more attention, and make more and more effort, to listen to God's word—especially when it is read, explained and discussed in the company of other believers.

3. Pray for right attitudes to hearing the word of God in your church, and practices which reflect these right attitudes.

6

Ecclesiastes 5:8-6:12; 8:1-17

The root of all meaninglessness

"Love of money", the apostle Paul says, "is a root of all kinds of evil". Perhaps Paul was reading Ecclesiastes in his quiet time when he penned those words, for here also the focus is on the love of money. As Ecclesiastes 5:10 says: "Whoever loves money never has money enough; whoever loves wealth is never satisfied with his income. This too is meaningless." Let's start by exploring why money figures in people's thinking when the issue of fulfilment in life is raised.

For Starters

1. Few would say that money itself gives them meaning in life. So why is money so important to so many people?

2. What are the effects on people of lack of money? Consider the personal and social effects as well as physical ones.

3. "Money is power." Discuss.

Although wealth and riches figure prominently in the central section of Ecclesiastes, the Teacher sees that there is a fundamental activity that gives rise to them, and a fundamental desire which can be met by having them. It is these fundamentals that need to be examined if there is to be any prospect of insight into the meaning of life through a consideration of money.

Investigate

Read Ecclesiastes 5:8-9.

1. What is the basic source of wealth (5:9)? What has to be done to get it?

2. Who will benefit from the activity of all? What privilege does he enjoy (cf. 8:2-4)?

3. What is the result of privileged position (5:8)? Why? What does this show is in the heart of man (cf. 6:7)?

The Teacher flags that the necessity of toil, and the desire for power, are fundamental driving forces in all that we do. And so both toil and power become important avenues by which we search for meaning in life. The Teacher therefore, by wisdom, analyses toil (5:8-6:12), and then power (chapter 8), to see whether they will yield the meaning of life. In between (in chapter 7), he analyses the wisdom he used to consider them, in an attempt to understand why his research has been so fruitless. We will deal with the central passage on wisdom in our next study.

The promise and disappointment of toil

Investigate

Read Ecclesiastes 5:8-6:12.

1. In 5:10-14, the Teacher analyses toil and the fruit of toil (wealth). Fill in the following table.

Analysis of toil by wisdom	What **promise** appears to be held out by toil or the fruit of toil (wealth)?	What bitter reality brings **disappointment** with the promise held out by toil?
5:10-11		
5:12		
5:13-14		

2. What is the bitter reality that brings ultimate disappointment to the promise of toil? (5:15-16)

3. The fruit of toil is eating, and life, which clearly are not bad things in themselves! Yet the impression given in 5:17 of the eating and life resulting from this toil is anything but positive. What makes it negative? What might the "darkness" be that the Teacher refers to?

4. Enjoyment of life and satisfaction in toil can nonetheless be experienced. Why? (5:18-20)

Verses 13-20 are another example of the Teacher looking around under the sun and seeing some things which are good and others which are evil. Overall the passage is tinged by a note of despair: our appetite to find truly fulfilling satisfaction and meaning will never be met, regardless of whether we are wise or foolish (6:7-9). The best we can do is settle for a surface satisfaction. We are utterly powerless to change this situation, and the more we try to plumb the depths of the impenetrability of meaning, the more it all feels meaningless, confirming our powerlessness. The reason for our powerlessness is that someone has barred us from finding ultimate meaning; someone who is more powerful than ourselves: God (6:10; see also 1:15). He may give us a degree of satisfaction, but when we ask questions about ultimate meaning we cannot find answers (6:12).

Before we further explore the reality of our powerlessness, let us take stock of the extent to which we think we experience real satisfaction in life. A good way of doing this is to consider how fulfilled we think we would be if certain things were removed from our lives.

Think it through

1. How much significance do you think your life would lose if you were to lose the following:

   - any enjoyment you get from the actual activity of the work you do

   - any satisfaction you get from seeing the results of the work you do

   - the esteem you are held in because of the work you do by family, friends, colleagues

   - any trappings your job might bring you: e.g. impressive title, nice office, flashy business card, desirable car, membership of exclusive clubs, etc., (depends on your job, of course!)

2. According to Ecclesiastes 5-6, which, if any, of the following factors determine whether people will gain satisfaction and enjoyment from their work?

- the job is highly paid

- the job has a high social status

- you are successful and have a good career path

- the job suits your personality and talents

3. Why is it that some people gain satisfaction and enjoyment in their work, and others don't?

4. Do you think you invest the work you do, or want to do, with more meaning than the writer of Ecclesiastes would deem wise? If so, how could you change your attitude?

The promise and disappointment of power

Toil leads to wealth, and wealth provides opportunity to exercise power. So the Teacher's inexorable logic leads him to a consideration of the promise and disappointment of power for finding the meaning of life.

Investigate

Read Ecclesiastes 8:1-17.

1. How does the advice of 8:2-6 relate to the truth expressed in 6:10?

2. What ultimately shows our powerlessness (8:7-8)?

3. The great leveller of death removes what little satisfaction might come from seeing those who abuse power suffer in their lifetimes for the injustice they cause to others. It also results in some wickedness never being uncovered (8:9-10). Nevertheless, what does the Teacher conclude is the "better" way to live under the sun, and why (8:12-13)?

The consideration of power leads the Teacher to return to a subject he noted at the beginning of this section of his book: the problem of injustice (5:8; 8:14). There is a hint of the ultimate accountability of all to God, but the overwhelming sense we are left with is of our inability to comprehend the exercise (or lack of exercise) of God's power in the face of blatant misuse of human power. It is this inability to understand that leads to the Teacher's conclusion in 8:15. It is not a cop out, so much as a capitulation to our powerlessness: all we can do is trust the only One who can—and does—give a sense of satisfaction to those whom he has nonetheless barred from discovering ultimate meaning in life. The Teacher expresses this conclusion most eloquently in 8:16-17, words which sum up the whole section covering toil, wisdom, and power, in 5:8-8:17.

We will further pursue the deep connection between these three ideas, and wickedness and death, in our next study. But it is worth noting at this point one New Testament passage which builds on the Teacher's insight into life under the sun, and sees his lessons as still applying to Christians today.

Think it through

After considering the hope of resurrection for believers in 1 Corinthians 15, the apostle Paul urges them in the final verse of the chapter to toil, knowing that their labour is not "in vain". The same word in Greek is used by Paul here as is used in the Greek version of Ecclesiastes, translated in the NIV as "meaningless".

1. The Teacher was wise enough to have identified a fundamental barrier which would stop us ever finding meaning. What was it (5:15-16)? How was power involved in it (8:7-8)?

Read 1 Corinthians 15:20-26, 50-58.

2. The believers that Paul is writing to know of something which addresses the barrier to finding meaning that the Teacher has identified. What is it? How is power involved in it?

3. Nevertheless, what must have been Paul's assumption about the experience of life for the believers in Corinth if he needs to write to them with a strong exhortation not to consider their toil to be in vain?

4. Why should we expect the Teacher's conclusions about toil to still be relevant to Christians, even though we live after Christ's resurrection?

Pray

1. Pray that you will have a right attitude to wealth. Thank God for whatever material well-being he has given you. Ask him to reveal to you ways in which you might put too much importance on financial security and the trappings of wealth. Pray that he will humble you in these areas (if you're game!).

2. Pray that you will have a right attitude to work and career. Thank God for whatever satisfaction you get from your work. Ask him to reveal to you ways in which you might be investing your work with more meaning than it can truly provide in "life under the sun". Pray that God will correct wrong attitudes and practices that flow from them.

3. Thank Jesus for the power over death he has demonstrated. Pray for a right view of what living for him will be like now, given that we still live "under the sun". Pray about particular areas where serving him seems futile, and you are tempted to give up.

7

Ecclesiastes 7

Why we can't find the meaning of life

We were left at the end of the last study with a devastating conclusion: meaning is inaccessible to us because God has barred us access to it; and because he is stronger than we are, there is no way we can overturn this situation. But surprisingly perhaps, there is comfort in this conclusion: the God who appears to be against us is also the God who can and does give us the ability to enjoy our meaningless lives, and even find a kind of satisfaction in the face of death. This comfort should prevent wise people from despairing–although it brings no guarantee. God can as easily withhold a sense of fulfilment from us as he can give it. We are totally dependent on his mercy.

The chapter we consider in this study spells out most clearly the reason why God has set things up this way. In it the Teacher takes us to the heart of the trio of ways used by mankind to seek meaning in life, ways which hold such promise and yet deliver such disappointment for the searcher. We have already considered the quest for meaning through power, and the quest for life without the despair brought by toil; now we turn to the quest for meaning through wisdom.

Investigate

Read Ecclesiastes 7:1-8.

1. What do wise people acknowledge is the ultimate reality about life?

2. How should this affect our overall attitude to life?

3. What attitude does the Teacher have to those who think life should, on the whole, be pleasurable? Why?

Read Ecclesiastes 7:9-19.

4. In what ways does the Teacher say we should not respond to the awfulness of realising our mortality (vv. 9-10)?

5. The Teacher commends wisdom as being of great benefit in facing the reality of life, but what are the limitations of wisdom (vv. 13-18)?

Think it through

1. How do we sanitise death and distance ourselves from it in Western society? Consider the extent of our direct contact with death, and how it is portrayed in the news media, film, soap-operas, and so on.

2. How much do you feel you have faced the reality of your mortality, and the mortality of people you love? Can facing up to death ever be an edifying experience?

3. What could wise Christians do to draw people's attention to the foolishness of pleasure-seeking? What might be people's reaction to Christians doing this?

4. We could react to the truth of 7:16-18 by saying, "I won't bother making any effort to pursue wisdom or live righteously". But the next observation of the Teacher in 7:19 prevents us from acting in this 'extreme' way. In what situations are you tempted to throw your hands up in the air and say, "This living-according-to-reality business is just too hard!" What potential benefits might come to you if you nonetheless pursue wisdom in these situations?

As much as the Teacher extols the benefits of wisdom over foolishness when facing up to the realities of life, he laments that even wisdom is powerless to penetrate the way God has made things in the present, or what the future holds. But why has God barred us access to comprehending the meaning of life? We have already read that it is "so that men will fear him" (in 3:14), but in the highly structured passage of 7:20-29 we learn even more.

Investigate

Read Ecclesiastes 7:20-29.

1. The question being addressed in this passage is placed right at the centre, with the answer and the evidence for it arranged like this:

    7:20 the underlying answer
        7:21-22 some evidence for this
            7:23-25 the question
        7:26-28 more evidence
    7:29 the underlying answer restated

Try to summarize each part:

    7:20 the answer:

        7:21-22 evidence:

            7:23-25 the question:

        7:26-28 more evidence:

    7:29 the answer restated:

2. Why is the world the way it is? Why has God barred us access to finding meaning?

Think it through

1. If mankind had remained in the original state of uprightness in which God had made us, what would we have not needed to do?

2. How is our search for meaning an expression of sin?

3. Religion is often described as a search for ultimate answers. In the light of Ecclesiastes and other passages in the Bible, someone has said, "All religion is rebellion". Do you agree?

There is a profound fittingness to God's action of frustrating our search for meaning, given that the search itself is an expression of our rejection of him. In our original state we had 'meaning' without having to do any searching, by virtue of our relationship to God as his creatures. And we had a clearly defined role in life, given to us by God to fulfil in the world he had created. It is worth considering the profound links between sin and the search for meaning expressed in the opening chapters of the Bible, and to note the contributions that toil, wisdom, and power made to creating the mess we are now in. (Skip this next 'Investigate' if you are short of time.)

Investigate

1. ***Read Genesis 2:7-9, 16-17.***

    a. How was right power and authority expressed in the world as God originally made it?

    b. How should this have been responded to in the man's "life under the sun"?

    c. If the man had lived according to the way God had made things—that is, wisely—what do you think would have been the result?

2. ***Read Genesis 3:1-5.***

    a. How is every aspect of this temptation an overturning of God's order of power and authority?

    b. How is it an expression of man's quest for power independent of God?

3. ***Read Genesis 3:6.***

    a. Why is the desire for wisdom not "better" in this context?

    b. How was the man's God-given work involved in his rebellion?

> 4. ***Read Genesis 3:17-23 and compare it to Genesis 2:7-9,15-17.***
>
> a. What is the consequence of mankind's rebellion against God? Who causes it?
>
> b. In particular, how does humanity's work change in nature after the rebellion?

As the early chapters of Genesis show us, there is now a rival to God in his world, another being who wants to determine what is good and what is evil. But the truth is that there is only one who is truly God. So the true God shows the false god his folly in two ways. Firstly, by denying him life (Gen 3:22b), which only the true God can create from nothing and sustain forever. And secondly, by frustrating the false god's presumption at being wise, i.e., at being able to set order in the universe and define the meaning of life.

Thus mankind's inability to remain alive, and our inability to fathom the meaning of life, are necessary consequences of presuming to be what we are not. When Adam and Eve did not presume to be gods, they could eat from the tree of life and live forever. They experienced the meaning of life as living in right relationship with their creator and his creation. The curses in Genesis 3 express God's denial of these privileges to mankind, and the book of Ecclesiastes explores how the reality of these curses is experienced in our daily lives. Again and again the Teacher brings us face to face with our mortality and the futility of our "life under the sun".

In many ways, Ecclesiastes is like an extended sermon with Genesis 3 as its text. The Teacher rams home the truth that we proud and sinful humans like to avoid—that we live in a cursed and frustrated world, are under the judgement of God, and that despite all our pretensions we cannot discover the meaning of it all.

In Genesis 3 there is a glimmer of hope. God graciously provides clothes for Adam and Eve, so that life can continue in a way that acknowledges that things are not as they were intended. And there is that fleeting hint in Genesis 3:15 that one day the "seed of the woman" will crush the serpent's head.

The New Testament rings with the truth that the 'one born of a woman' has indeed come, and defeated Satan and all his powers. And even though the creation is still "subjected to futility", it now waits in eager expectation for its liberation from that state into the "glorious freedom of the children of God" (Rom 8:20-21). In the gospel of Jesus Christ we have the promise that the groaning and frustration so vividly portrayed in Ecclesiastes will soon come to an end.

Think it through

Read Romans 8:18-25.

1. In what ways does this passage indicate that "life under the sun" is still a frustrating and difficult business?

2. How is the hope of the future described in Romans 8? What should we do in the meantime?

3. Thinking back over Ecclesiastes (and Romans 8), how should we regard suffering and difficulty in our lives as Christians?

Pray

1. It is a remarkable privilege to be born at this time in history, on this side of the life, death, and resurrection of Jesus. Spend some time in prayer thanking God for the privilege of knowing how he has dealt with the mortality and futility that we should feel in life because of our sin. Thank Jesus for dealing with the problem of our rebellious quest to be like God in wisdom, power and self-sustaining life.

2. Pray that God will help you live in the "fear of God", to use the Teacher's language. Pray about particular areas of your life in which you are tempted to strive for life, power, and wisdom without acknowledging God.

3. Pray that members of your church will have a realistic view of the struggle that is the Christian life while "under the sun", and help support one another in the struggle, rather than deny its reality.

8

Ecclesiastes 9:1–11:6

Why we should live life to the full

Ecclesiastes deals with the God-given desire humans have to plumb the meaning of life, our quest to find the reason why things are the way they are in the universe, and what our place is in it. But after much research, the Teacher concludes that no matter how hard we try, no matter how much brain-power, technology or money we throw at the quest, we will always draw a blank and be denied a satisfying answer. As he puts it in 8:16-17:

> When I applied my mind to know wisdom and to observe man's labour on earth—his eyes not seeing sleep day or night—then I saw all that God has done. No-one can comprehend what goes on under the sun. Despite all his efforts to search it out, man cannot discover its meaning. Even if a wise man claims he knows, he cannot really comprehend it.

As we have seen, the ultimate reason for this is that God frustrates our attempts to find meaning, so that in our sinfulness and pride we might be humbled before him, and learn to fear him.

For Starters

1. Some of us will have heard an elderly person say, "The only thing I know is that I know nothing". What might someone be meaning when they say this?

2. Is the Teacher meaning what these people mean when he says similar words e.g. 1:17; 7:23-4; 8:17? What might he be saying about the human condition that is far more profound than is usually meant by people who say they know nothing?

What should be our response to this realisation of the way things really are? Ecclesiastes 9:1-11:6 answers that question. The Teacher reports more things in life which show us our inability to understand the world God has made–things which show the impossibility of our comprehending the world. In previous chapters the Teacher has reported the despair this realisation has brought him (e.g. 1:18; 2:20), and he has commended such despair as an expression of wisdom (7:4) because it acknowledges the way things really are. Yet each time he has not spiralled into a state of irretrievable depression. Rather, he has gone on to commend finding satisfaction and gladness while living the meaningless life (e.g. 2:24-25; 3:13; 5:18).

In chapter 9 through to 11:6, the Teacher shows what this will mean in a whole range of areas of life, and what we should realistically expect in life. We will investigate and think through these chapters in three sections.

1. Enjoy your meaningless life

Investigate

Read Ecclesiastes 9:1-10.

1. The Teacher returns to a familiar theme in verses 1-3. What event renders life so meaningless?

2. How would you summarize the conclusion he draws from this in verses 4-10?

Think it through

1. Ecclesiastes 9:1-10 could be summed up by the advice: "Live life to the full while you have it–even if you don't know why". Bringing God into the assessment of things (vv. 7,9) leads to this recommendation, rather than to the recommendation of lying down to die. Why should acknowledging God's involvement in denying us knowledge have this positive effect?

2. Where would you plot yourself, and your church fellowship, on a scale showing attitude to life under the sun?

Despair of life		Balanced		Live life to the full
1	2	3	4	5

3. Is it possible to experience the attitudes at both ends of the scale simultaneously? Which do you think is better: to have a balanced approach to life, or one holding two extremes at the same time? What do you think the Teacher would recommend?

2. Watch what you're doing

Investigate

Read Ecclesiastes 9:11-10:20.

1. What further evidence does the Teacher put forward to show that the world is strange and incomprehensible?

    9:11-12

    9:13-16

    10:1

2. All the same, the Teacher says being wise is still better than being foolish. Look back over chapter 10 and note:

    a. things about life that the wise understand and act on

    b. how the fool acts, and what happens to him

3. You would hope that those whose job it is to lead and rule people would have wisdom. That at least would be the right order of things (consider Solomon's prayer and God's response in 1 Kings 3:7-10). What does the Teacher say we should expect (see 9:17-18; 10:4-7; 10:16-17)?

Think it through

1. Do you think people have too high expectations of politicians? What about the Royal Family?

2. Ecclesiastes 10:2 is not a comment on political alignment–the Teacher could have made the point equally as well by swapping 'right' and 'left'. His point is that wisdom or foolishness is not always obvious from the actual decision made, but becomes apparent in the subsequent course of life (see 10:3). Can you think of examples of this?

3. How do you rate according to the characteristics of wisdom and foolishness in this chapter? What practical changes could you make to your life?

3. The wise risk-taker

Don't despair, says the Teacher. Even though life is impossible to fully understand, you should still live it to the full. And this means taking calculated risks.

Investigate

Read Ecclesiastes 11:1-6.

1. What do the actions described in verses 1-2 have in common? What attitudes might motivate these actions?

2. Why can we know with certainty and act with confidence upon the things described in verse 3? The illustrations in verses 4-5 contrast this certainty. What conclusion does the Teacher want us to draw from considering these matters?

3. What should our ignorance lead us to do?

Think it through

1. Fear of taking risks can stop us getting involved in life. In what areas of life are you a risk-taker? In what areas are you not?

2. People can show foolishness by taking many risks, or by taking few risks. How does Ecclesiastes 10 and 11 bear this out? Which expression of foolishness do you tend towards?

3. The Teacher commends a willingness to get involved in life despite not understanding it or what the future holds. How can such a willingness demonstrate a right acknowledgement of God and an appropriately humble view of self?

4. How might this passage affect your attitude to life? In what practical areas might this be expressed?

The material in chapters 9-11 of Ecclesiastes seems quite varied, but there is a common thread running through it. It commends the only wise response to the reality of life "under the sun": the response of faith. The word 'faith' is not mentioned in Ecclesiastes–but the idea is at the heart of the notion of 'fearing God', which occurs on three important occasions in the book (7:18; 8:13; 12:13). We show faith by living "under the sun" with no expectation that God has to explain himself to us; we show faith by not giving in to paralysing despair just because we cannot understand the strange twists and turns of life. Faith recognizes that we are creatures totally dependent on our Creator, and gets on with living and enjoying life to the full in his creation.

Think it through

1. How do the following New Testament passages confirm (and expand on) the Teacher's findings?

   2 Corinthians 5:4-7

   Hebrews 11:1-6

   1 Corinthians 3:18-23

   Romans 8:23-27

2. How willing are you to hear that your desire to plumb the deep meaning of things will always be frustrated?

3. What sort of experiences in life, or education background, make it hard for people to accept the perspective of Ecclesiastes–that things need to be accepted purely on the basis of faith, and not by sight?

Pray

1. Pray that you will be someone who increasingly is willing to live by faith, without demanding sight to make sense of life.

2. Pray that God will give you the wisdom to take appropriate risks in dependence upon him, and avoid foolish ones which are an expression of pride. Pray about particular decisions you have to make.

9

Ecclesiastes 11:7-12:14

The end of the matter

We finally reach the end of the book of Ecclesiastes, and the "end of the matter", as far as the Teacher is concerned. He has conducted his extensive investigation. He has gone about seeing all that is done "under the sun". And as he draws it all to a close, he considers the full span of our lives–from birth to death.

Investigate

Read Ecclesiastes 11:7-10.

1. Why is it good for young people to enjoy life?

2. What warning does the Teacher give young people as they pursue life vigorously?

THE SEARCH FOR MEANING • 65

3. What then should be the twofold attitude to life of the young person?
Translation note: It may help in answering this question to realise that 11:10 reads literally: "Therefore, remove sorrow (or vexation) from your heart, and put away evil from your flesh" (see KJV, RV).

Now read Ecclesiastes 12:1-8.

4. The Teacher turns from a consideration of youth to the inevitable process of ageing. How do verses 1-7 convey the realities of old age and death?

5. How does verse 8 relate to verse 7?

Think it through

1. What indications are there in our society that we live in a culture which worships youth and youthfulness? What would the Teacher say to this?

2. What strategies are used in our society to avoid facing the realities of ageing and death?

3. At the risk of generalisation, how much do you think God figures in the thinking of people in our society:

   a. when they are young?

   b. in old age?

4. Think back over the message of Ecclesiastes. Why does the inevitable reality of ageing and death render life 'meaningless' from our point of view?

The conclusion

With the refrain of "meaningless, meaningless" ringing in our ears, we come to the final concluding summary or epilogue, in 12:9-14. Perhaps here we will find some answer that the Teacher has been holding back, some gem of insight that will leave us encouraged that everything is not so "meaningless" after all.

Not so. The Teacher gives us no relief. He says that the conclusion of all his investigation is simply this: Fear God, and keep his commandments, for this is the whole duty of man (v. 13).

For modern readers, this is almost a let down. We want an upbeat, feelgood ending that will dispel the clouds of gloom. And even if the Teacher won't or can't give us a more satisfying answer, we want a clue as to where we might go for further study and investigation so as to finally crack the puzzle. Verses 9-12 highlight how foolish this is. The Teacher was one of the wisest men who ever lived. We may not like his conclusions; they may irritate us, in fact, like goads. But we shouldn't think that by more study we will somehow solve the problem that the Teacher has been unable to solve. No-one ever has. Of all the millions of books that have been written since the Teacher wrote his, none have been able to answer his fundamental problem.

This, of course, is for the reason that the Teacher has already stated a number of times–God has prevented us from ever solving this problem. It is God himself who has subjected the world to the futility in which it currently groans; he is the one who prevents humanity from ever understanding the meaning of the events of life, or from knowing what will happen next. God has done this so that we will fear him.

The Teacher's conclusion, then, is that which he has been saying all along. Given that we cannot comprehend the meaning of all the strange and apparently contradictory events of life, only one course of action is open to us:

- enjoy the good things that do come our way with thankfulness to God;
- accept the reality of bad things happening, and the fact that we cannot find out why;
- fear God, and obey his commandments.

This is wisdom. This is living according to reality–the reality of being striving beings whom God has frustrated. Let us conclude by thinking how it applies to us as Christians, living this side of the death and resurrection of Christ.

Think it through

1. How is our situation different to the Teacher's, given that we live this side of Christ? Consider again Romans 8:18-25. Are we more able than the Teacher to explain the meaninglessness of life under the sun?

2. How is our situation still the same as the Teacher's, despite us living this side of Christ? How will Ecclesiastes help us live in this world?

3. Look up Luke 12:4-5.

   a. What does Jesus mean by his command to "fear God"?

   b. Do you fear God the way Jesus means? Why/why not?

   c. Do you think modern Christians fear God? How is this demonstrated?

   d. How is this exhortation to fear God generally received by Westerners today?

4. Read 1 Corinthians 1:18-21,27-29. How is Paul's message to the Corinthian Christians consistent with the Teacher's message to his readers?

5. How would the Teacher react to the following attitudes found in some Christian circles today:

   a. that if you are good, God will bless you with prosperity and health; and that poverty and sickness are the result of sin and lack of faith

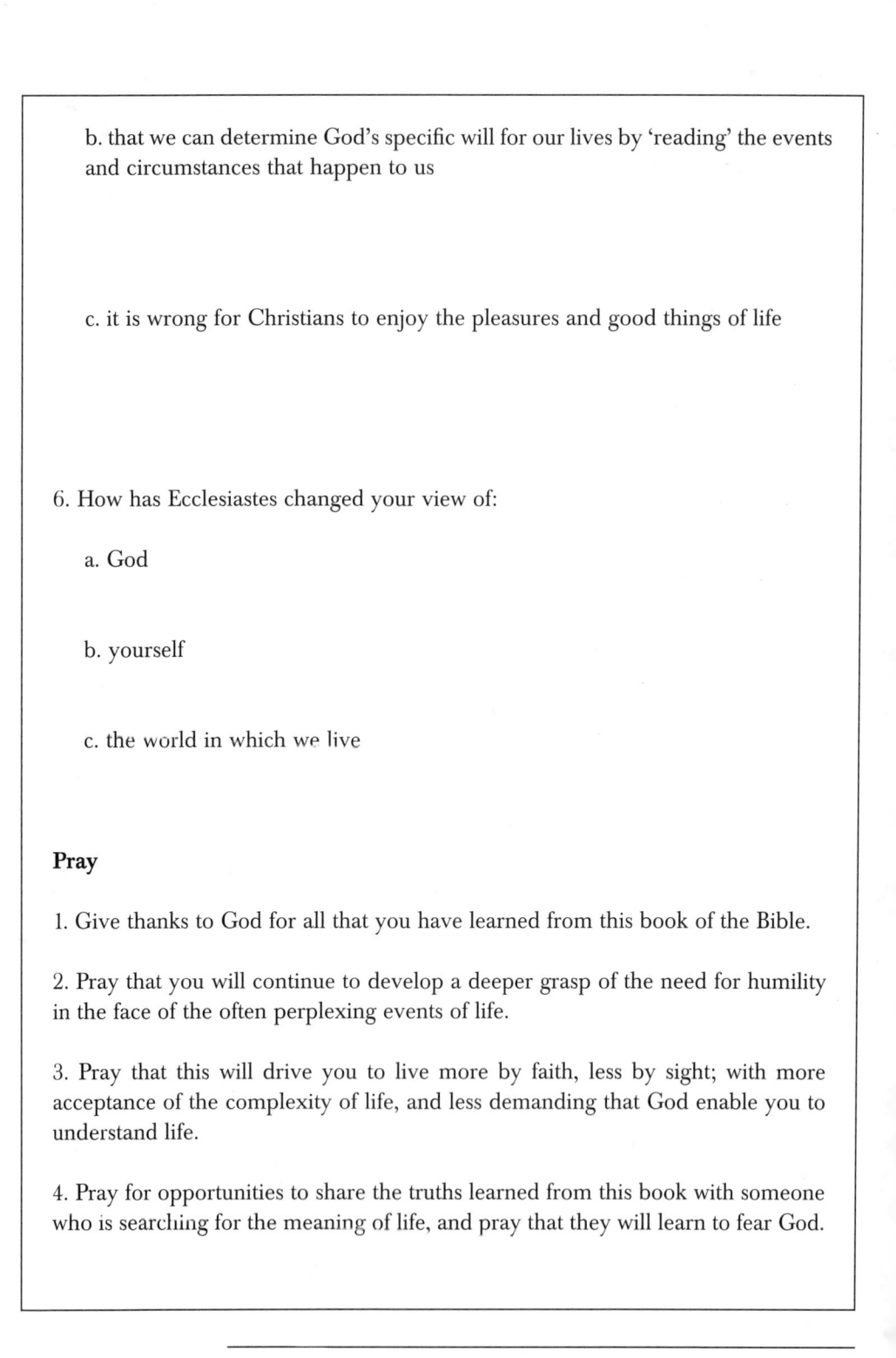

b. that we can determine God's specific will for our lives by 'reading' the events and circumstances that happen to us

c. it is wrong for Christians to enjoy the pleasures and good things of life

6. How has Ecclesiastes changed your view of:

a. God

b. yourself

c. the world in which we live

Pray

1. Give thanks to God for all that you have learned from this book of the Bible.

2. Pray that you will continue to develop a deeper grasp of the need for humility in the face of the often perplexing events of life.

3. Pray that this will drive you to live more by faith, less by sight; with more acceptance of the complexity of life, and less demanding that God enable you to understand life.

4. Pray for opportunities to share the truths learned from this book with someone who is searching for the meaning of life, and pray that they will learn to fear God.

The Good Book Company

Who are we?
Ever since we opened our doors in 1991 as St Matthias Press, our aim has been to provide the Christian community with products of a uniformly high standard—both in their biblical faithfulness and in the quality of the writing and production.

Now known as The Good Book Company, we have grown to become an international provider of user-friendly resources, many of them from Matthias Media, with Christians of all sorts using our Bible studies, books, Briefings, audio cassettes, videos, training courses and daily Bible reading resources.

Buy direct or from your local bookshop
You can order your resources either direct from us, or from your local Christian bookshop. There are advantages in both, but if you buy from us, you get these benefits:
- you save time—we usually despatch our orders within 24 hours of receiving them
- you save money—we have built-in discounts for bulk buying.
- you help keep us afloat—because we get more from each sale, buying from us direct helps us to invest more time and energy in providing you with the very best resources.

Please call us for a free catalogue of all our resources, including an up-to-date list of other titles in this Interactive Bible Studies series. Some details of IBS titles are contained on the following page.

Phone: 020-8942-0880

Address: Elm House, 37 Elm Road, New Malden, Surrey KT3 3HB

FAX: 020-8942-0990 (pay by credit card or invoice)

Email: admin@thegoodbook.co.uk
Website: www.thegoodbook.co.uk

Interactive and Topical Bible Studies

Our Interactive Bible Studies (IBS) and Topical Bible Studies (TBS) are a valuable resource to help you keep feeding from God's Word. The IBS series works through passages and books of the Bible; the TBS series pulls together the Bible's teaching on topics, such as money or prayer. As at October 2001, the series contains the following titles:

OLD TESTAMENT

FULL OF PROMISE
(THE BIG PICTURE OF THE O.T.)
Authors: Phil Campbell
& Bryson Smith, 8 studies

BEYOND EDEN (GENESIS 1-11)
Authors: Phillip Jensen
and Tony Payne, 9 studies

THE ONE AND ONLY
(DEUTERONOMY)
Author: Bryson Smith,
8 studies

THE GOOD, THE BAD & THE UGLY (JUDGES)
Author: Mark Baddeley
10 studies

FAMINE & FORTUNE (RUTH)
Authors: Barry Webb &
David Hohne, 4 studies

THE EYE OF THE STORM (JOB)
Author: Bryson Smith,
6 studies

THE SEARCH FOR MEANING
(ECCLESIASTES)
Author: Tim McMahon,
9 studies

TWO CITIES (ISAIAH)
Authors: Andrew Reid and
Karen Morris, 9 studies

KINGDOM OF DREAMS
(DANIEL)
Authors: Andrew Reid and
Karen Morris, 8 studies

BURNING DESIRE
(OBADIAH & MALACHI)
Authors: Phillip Jensen and
Richard Pulley, 6 studies

NEW TESTAMENT

THE GOOD LIVING GUIDE
(MATTHEW 5:1-12)
Authors: Phillip Jensen
and Tony Payne, 9 studies

NEWS OF THE HOUR (MARK)
Author: Peter Bolt,
10 studies

FREE FOR ALL (GALATIANS)
Authors: Phillip Jensen
& Kel Richards, 8 studies

WALK THIS WAY (EPHESIANS)
Author: Bryson Smith,
8 studies

THE COMPLETE CHRISTIAN
(COLOSSIANS)
Authors: Phillip Jensen
and Tony Payne, 8 studies

ALL LIFE IS HERE (1 TIM)
Authors: Phillip Jensen
and Greg Clarke, 9 studies

RUN THE RACE (2 TIM)
Author: Bryson Smith,
6 studies

THE PATH TO GODLINESS
(TITUS)
Authors: Phillip Jensen
and Tony Payne, 6 studies

FROM SHADOW TO REALITY
(HEBREWS)
Author: Joshua Ng,
9 studies

THE IMPLANTED WORD
(JAMES)
Authors: Phillip Jensen
and K.R. Birkett, 8 studies

HOMEWARD BOUND (1 PETER)
Authors: Phillip Jensen and
Tony Payne, 10 studies

ALL YOU NEED TO KNOW
(2 PETER)
Author: Bryson Smith,
6 studies

TOPICAL BIBLE STUDIES

BOLD I APPROACH
(PRAYER)
Author: Tony Payne,
6 studies

CASH VALUES
(MONEY)
Author: Tony Payne,
5 studies

THE BLUEPRINT
(DOCTRINE)
Authors: Phillip Jensen
& Tony Payne, 11 studies

WOMAN OF GOD
Author: Terry Blowes
8 studies

THE MAN WHO MAKES A DIFFERENCE (EPHESIANS)
Author: Tony Payne
7 studies
This set of studies from Ephesians, is designed especially for men, and is sold as a separate leaders' guide and study guide

---

For an up-to date list visit:
www.thegoodbook.co.uk
or call 020-8942-0880